20 FAVORITE SONGS

Disney

SONGS FOR BARITONE UKULELE

ISBN 978-1-4950-8695-3

The following songs are the property of:
Bourne Co.
Music Publishers
5 West 37th Street
New York, NY 10018

HEIGH-HO • SOME DAY MY PRINCE WILL COME • WHEN YOU WISH UPON A STAR
WHISTLE WHILE YOU WORK • WHO'S AFRAID OF THE BIG BAD WOLF?

7777 W. BLUEMOUND RD. P.O. BOX 13819 MILWAUKEE, WI 53213

Visit Hal Leonard Online at
www.halleonard.com

UKULELE NOTATION LEGEND

THE MUSICAL STAFF shows pitches and rhythms and is divided by bar lines into measures. Pitches are named after the first seven letters of the alphabet.

TABLATURE graphically represents the ukulele fingerboard. Each horizontal line represents a a string, and each number represents a fret.

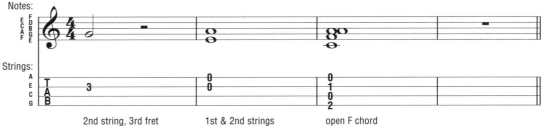

2nd string, 3rd fret   1st & 2nd strings open, played together   open F chord

HALF-STEP BEND: Strike the note and bend up 1/2 step.

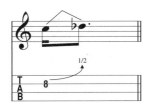

WHOLE-STEP BEND: Strike the note and bend up one step.

GRACE NOTE BEND: Strike the note and immediately bend up as indicated.

SLIGHT (MICROTONE) BEND: Strike the note and bend up 1/4 step.

BEND AND RELEASE: Strike the note and bend up as indicated, then release back to the original note. Only the first note is struck.

PRE-BEND: Bend the note as indicated, then strike it.

VIBRATO: The string is vibrated by rapidly bending and releasing the note with the fretting hand.

HAMMER-ON: Strike the first (lower) note with one finger, then sound the higher note (on the same string) with another finger by fretting it without picking.

PULL-OFF: Place both fingers on the notes to be sounded. Strike the first note and without picking, pull the finger off to sound the second (lower) note.

LEGATO SLIDE: Strike the first note and then slide the same fret-hand finger up or down to the second note. The second note is not struck.

SHIFT SLIDE: Same as legato slide, except the second note is struck.

TRILL: Very rapidly alternate between the notes indicated by continuously hammering on and pulling off.

TREMOLO PICKING: The note is picked as rapidly and continuously as possible.

NOTE: Tablature numbers in parentheses mean:

1. The note is being sustained over a system (note in standard notation is tied), or

2. The note is sustained, but a new articulation (such as a hammer-on, pull-off, slide or vibrato) begins, or

3. The note is a barely audible "ghost" note (note in standard notation is also in parentheses).

Additional Musical Definitions

 (accent)   • Accentuate note (play it louder)

 (staccato)   • Play the note short

D.S. al Coda   • Go back to the sign (𝄋), then play until the measure marked "*To Coda*," then skip to the section labelled "*Coda*."

D.C. al Fine   • Go back to the beginning of the song and play until the measure marked "*Fine*" (end).

N.C.   • No chord.

    • Repeat measures between signs.

• When a repeated section has different endings, play the first ending only the first time and the second ending only the second time.

Alice in Wonderland

from ALICE IN WONDERLAND
Words by Bob Hilliard
Music by Sammy Fain

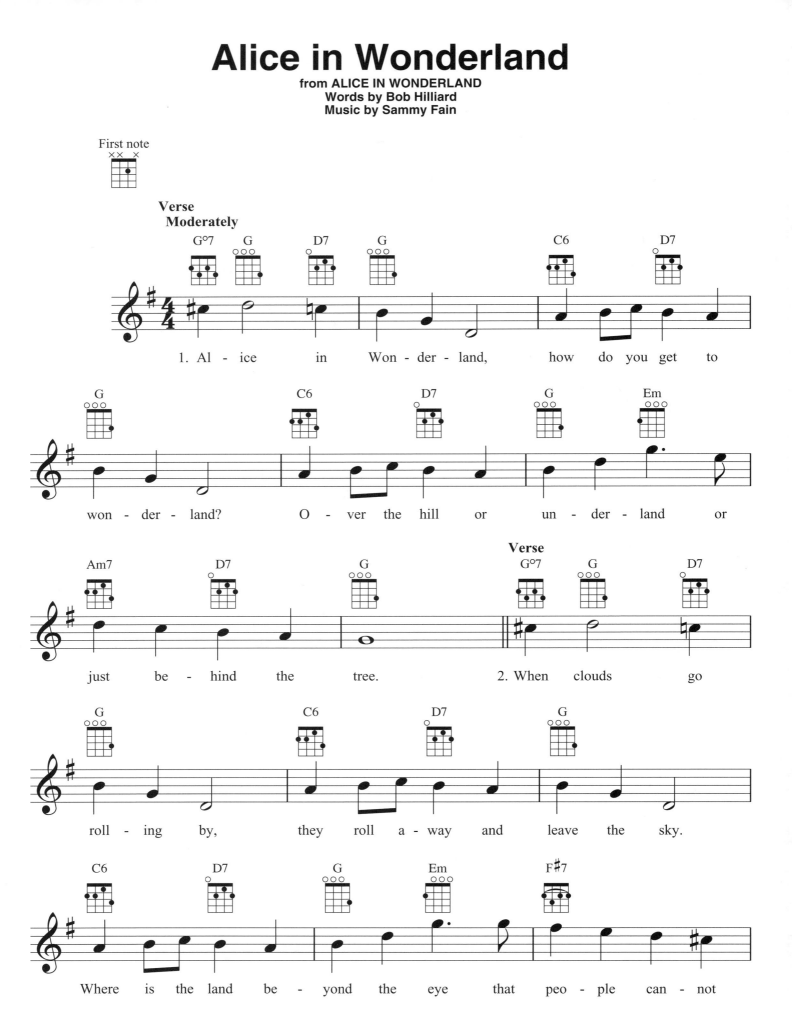

Bridge

see? _____ Where can it be? Where do stars go? Where is the cres - cent moon? They must be some - where in the sun - ny af - ter -

Verse

noon. 3. Al - ice in Won - der - land, where is the path to Won - der - land? O - ver the hill or here or there? I won - der where.

The Bare Necessities

from THE JUNGLE BOOK
Words and Music by Terry Gilkyson

Look for the bare ne-ces-si-ties, __ the sim-ple bare ne-ces-si-ties; __ for-get a-bout your wor-ries and your strife.

(1.,3.) I mean the bare ne-ces-si-ties, __ or Moth-er Na-ture's
(2.) I mean the bare ne-ces-si-ties, __ that's why a bear can

rec-i-pes __ that bring the bare ne-ces-si-ties __ of life.
rest at ease __ with just the bare ne-ces-si-ties __ of life.

1. Wher-ev-er I wan-der, _____ wher-ev-er I roam,
2. When you __ pick a paw-paw _____ or pric-kl-y pear,
3. So just try to re-lax (Spoken:) Oh yeah! in my back-yard.

I could - n't be fond - er _____ of my big home.
and you __ prick a raw paw, _____ next time be - ware.
If you act like that bee acts, _____ you're work-in' too hard.

The bees are buzz-in' in the tree to make some hon-ey just for
Don't pick the prick-ly pear by paw. When you pick a pear, try to use the
Don't spend your time just look-in' a - round for some-thing you want that can't be

me. You look un-der the rocks and plants and take a glance at the
claw. But you don't need to use the claw when you pick a pear of the
found. When you find out you can live with-out it and go a-long not

fan - cy ants, __ then may-be try a few. ⎫
big paw - paw. __ Have I giv - en you a clue? ⎬ The bare ne-
think-in' a - bout __ it, I'll tell you some-thing true: ⎭

ces - si - ties of life will come to you, they'll come to

1., 2.

you! Look for the

3.

you! _____

7

Beauty and the Beast

from BEAUTY AND THE BEAST
Music by Alan Menken
Lyrics by Howard Ashman

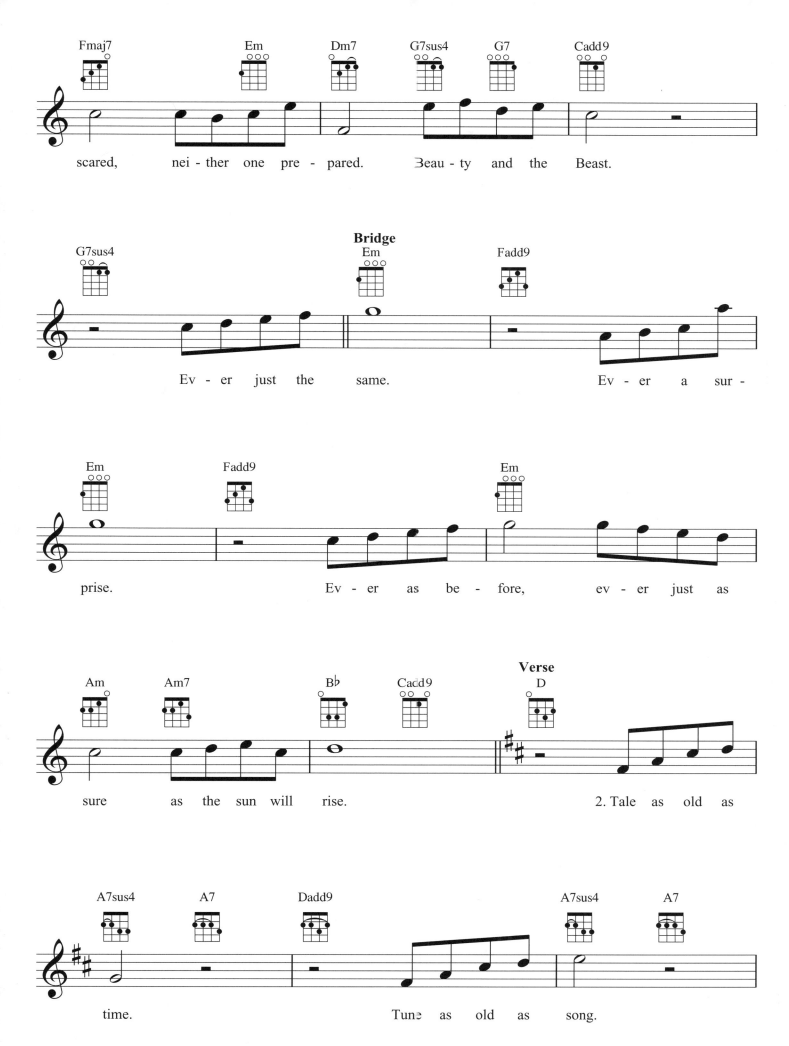

scared,   nei - ther one pre - pared.   Beau - ty and the Beast.

Bridge

Ev - er just the same.   Ev - er a sur -

prise.   Ev - er as be - fore,   ev - er just as

Verse

sure   as the sun will rise.   2. Tale as old as

time.   Tune as old as song.

9

Chim Chim Cher-ee

from MARY POPPINS
Words and Music by Richard M. Sherman and Robert B. Sherman

Bibbidi-Bobbidi-Boo
(The Magic Song)

from CINERELLA
Words by Jerry Livingston
Music by Mack David and Al Hoffman

Verse
Moderately

1. Sa - la - ga - doo - la men - chic - ka boo - la

bib - bi - di - bob - bi - di - boo. Put 'em to - geth - er and what have you got?

Verse

Bib - bi - di - bob - bi - di - boo.

2. Sa - la - ga - doo - la men - chic - ka boo - la

bib - bi - di - bob - bi - di - boo. It - 'll do mag - ic, be - lieve it or not,

Can You Feel the Love Tonight

from THE LION KING
Music by Elton John
Lyrics by Tim Rice

Candle on the Water

from PETE'S DRAGON
Words and Music by Al Kasha and Joel Hirschhorn

cir - cling in the air, light - ed by a prayer. _____

Verse

3. I'll be your can - dle on the wa - ter. This flame in - side of me will

grow. Keep hold - ing on; you'll make it. Here's my hand, so take it.

Outro

Look for me reach - ing out to show as sure as riv - ers flow,

I'll nev - er let you go. I'll nev - er let you go.

I'll nev - er let you go. _____

Circle of Life

from THE LION KING
Music by Elton John
Lyrics by Tim Rice

on the path un-wind - ing

in the cir-

To Coda

1.

- cle, _____ the cir - cle of life. _____

2.

D.S. al Coda

the cir - cle of life! _____

Coda

the cir - cle of life. _____

Outro

On the path un-wind - ing

in the cir - cle, _____

the cir - cle of life. _____

Heigh-Ho

The Dwarfs' Marching Song from SNOW WHITE AND THE SEVEN DWARFS
Words by Larry Morey
Music by Frank Churchill

It's a Small World

from Disney Parks' "it's a small world" attraction
Words and Music by Richard M. Sherman and Robert B. Sherman

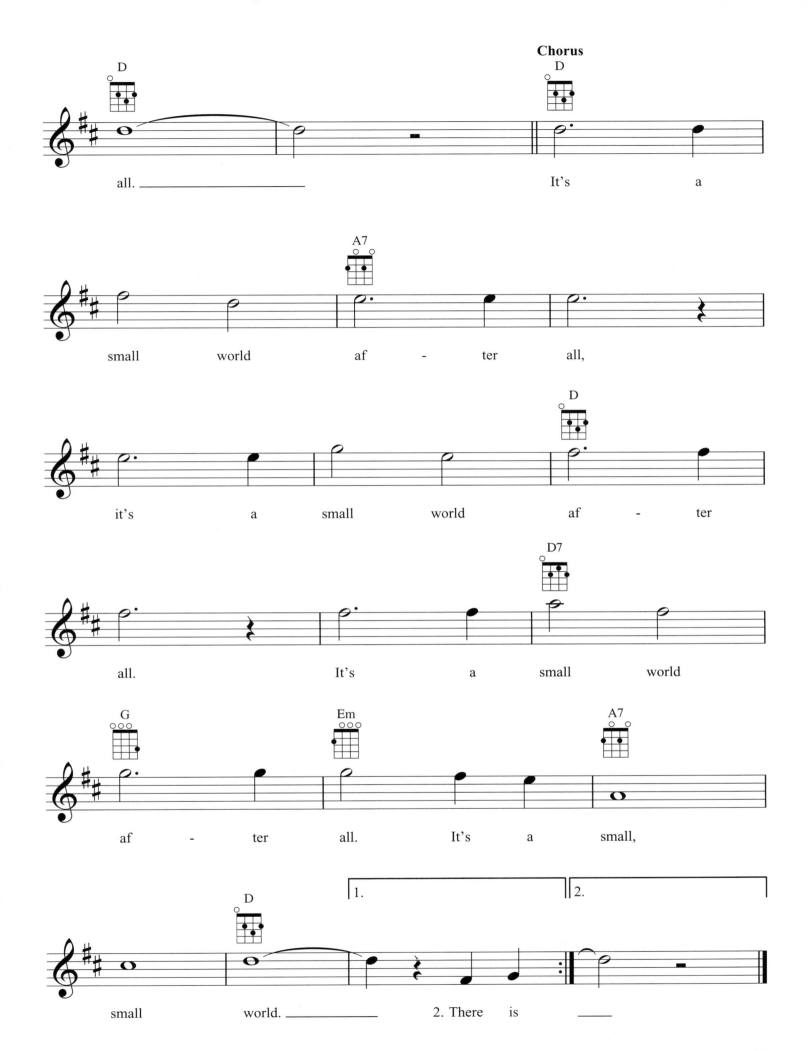

Chorus

all. _____ It's a small world af - ter all, it's a small world af - ter all. It's a small world af - ter all. It's a small, small world. _____ 2. There is _____

Let It Go

from FROZEN

Music and Lyrics by Kristen Anderson-Lopez and Robert Lopez

let it go; _____ can't _____
let it go; _____ I am

hold it back an - y - more. _____ Let it go, _____
one with the wind and sky. _____ Let it go, _____

let it go; _____ turn a - way _____
let it go; _____ you'll _____ nev -

_____ and slam _____ the _____ door. _____
- er see _____ me cry. _____

I don't _ care _____ what they're going to _____ say: _____
Here I _____ stand _____ and here I'll _____ stay; _____

To Coda ⊕

let the storm rage _____ on. _____

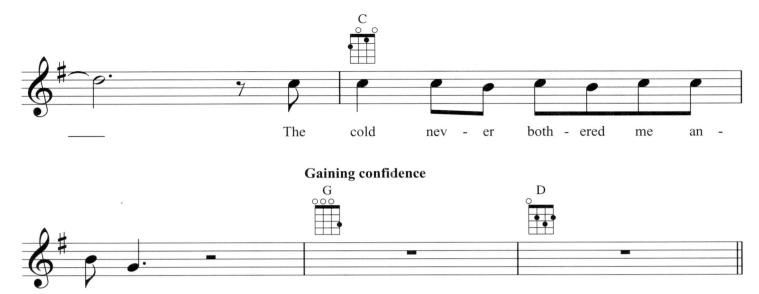

The cold nev - er both - ered me an -

Gaining confidence

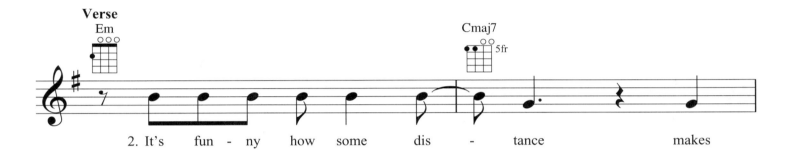

y - way.

Verse

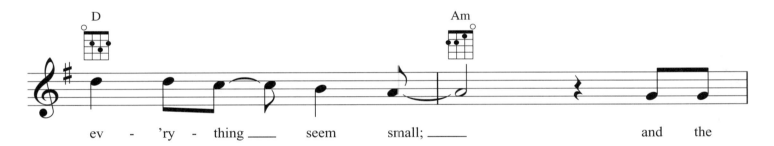

2. It's fun - ny how some dis - tance makes

ev - 'ry - thing __ seem small; __ and the

fears that once __ con - trolled __ me can't

Pre-Chorus

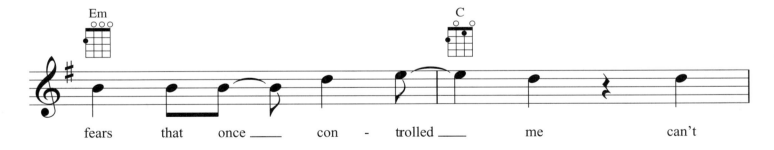

get to me __ at all. __ It's time __ to see __

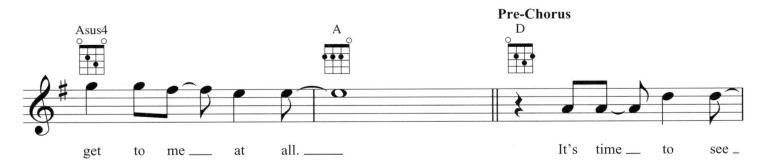

-ral - ing _____ in fro - zen frac - tals all _____

_____ a - round. _____ And one _____ thought crys -

- tal - liz - es like _____ an i - cy blast: _____

I'm nev - er go - ing back; _____ the

past is in _____ the past! _____ Let it go, _____

Chorus

_____ let it go, _____ and I'll rise _____

31

Mickey Mouse March

from THE MICKEY MOUSE CLUB
Words and Music by Jimmie Dodd

Some Day My Prince Will Come

from SNOW WHITE AND THE SEVEN DWARFS

Words by Larry Morey
Music by Frank Churchill

First note

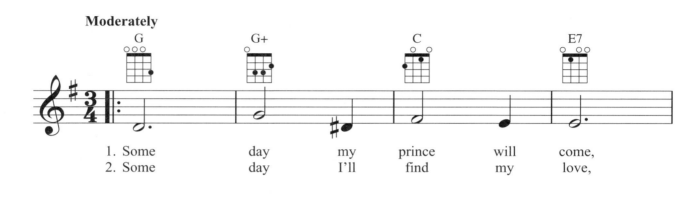

1. Some day my prince will come,
2. Some day I'll find will my love,

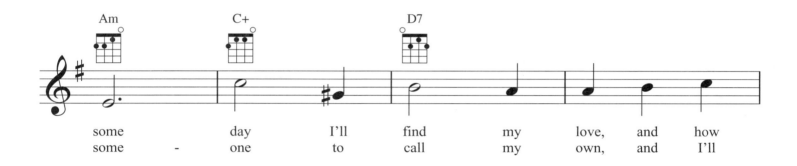

some day I'll find my love, and how
some - one to call my own, and I'll

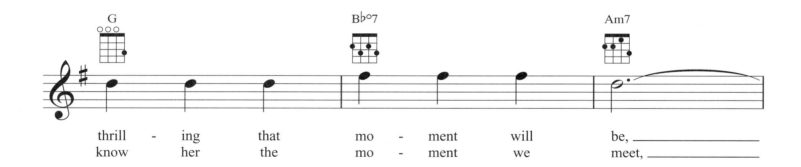

thrill - ing that mo - ment will be, ___
know her the mo - ment we meet, ___

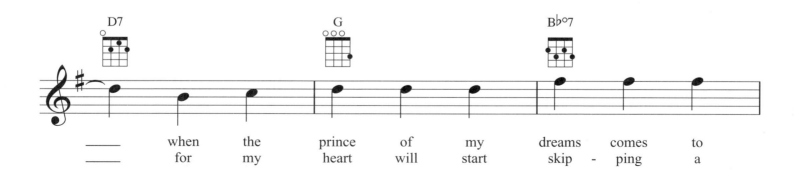

___ when the prince of my dreams comes to
___ for my heart will start skip - ping a

me. _____

beat. _____

He'll whis - per

Some day we'll

"I love you" And steal a

say and do things we've been

kiss or two. Though he's } far a - way, I'll

long - ing to. Though she's }

find my love some day, some day when my dreams come

1.

true. _____

2.

true. _____

Supercalifragilisticexpialidocious

from MARY POPPINS

Words and Music by Richard M. Sherman and Robert B. Sherman

First note

Chorus
Moderately fast, in 2

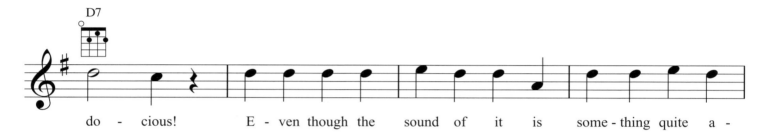

Su - per - cal - i - frag - il - is - tic - ex - pi - al - i -

do - cious! E - ven though the sound of it is some - thing quite a -

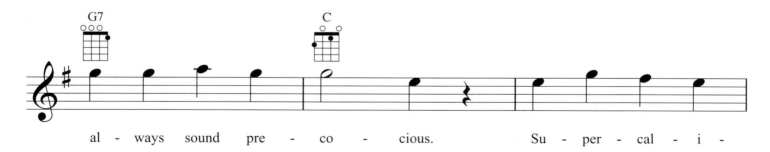

tro - cious, if you say it loud e - nough, you'll

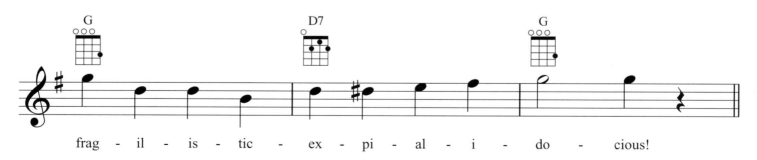

al - ways sound pre - co - cious. Su - per - cal - i -

frag - il - is - tic - ex - pi - al - i - do - cious!

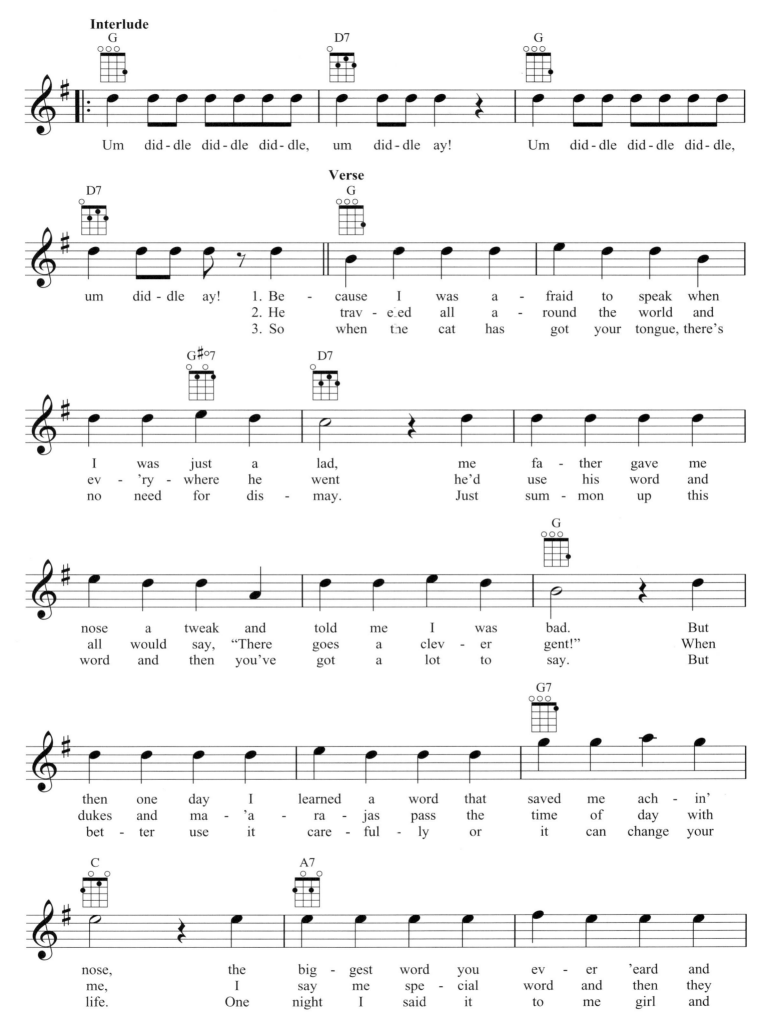

When She Loved Me

from TOY STORY 2

Music and Lyrics by Randy Newman

she loved me. Through the sum - mer and the fall, we

had each oth - er, that was all. Just she and I to - geth - er, like

it was meant to be. And when she was lone - ly, I was there to com - fort her, and I

knew _____ that she loved me.

Bridge

So the years went by; I stayed the same. But she be - gan to drift a - way;

I was left a - lone. Still I wait - ed for the day

When You Wish Upon a Star

from PINOCCHIO
Words by Ned Washington
Music by Leigh Harline

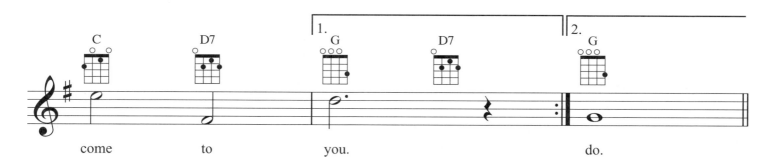

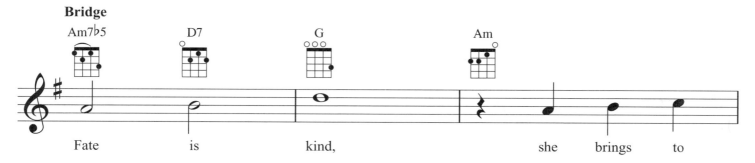

Whistle While You Work

from SNOW WHITE AND THE SEVEN DWARFS
Words by Larry Morey
Music by Frank Churchill

First note

Verse
Moderately

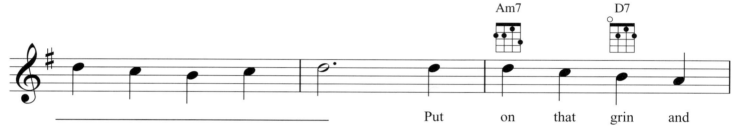

1. Just whis - tle while you work. _Whistle_ ____

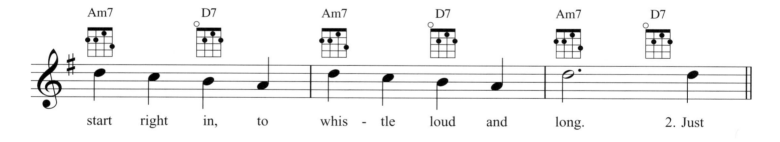

____ Put on that grin and

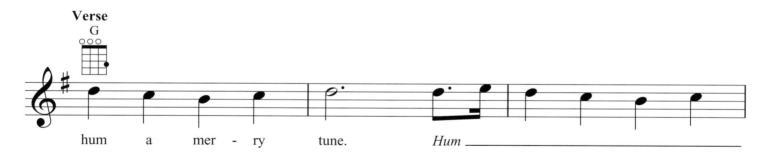

start right in, to whis - tle loud and long. 2. Just

Verse

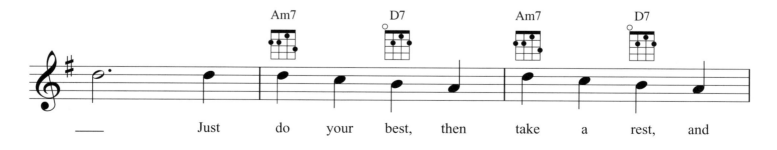

hum a mer - ry tune. _Hum_ ____

____ Just do your best, then take a rest, and

sing your - self a song. When there's too much to

do, don't let it both - er you. For -

get your trou - ble, try to be just like the cheer - ful

chick - a - dee, and whis - tle while you work. *Whistle* ___

Come on, get smart, tune

up and start to whis - tle while you work.

Who's Afraid of the Big Bad Wolf?

from THREE LITTLE PIGS
Words and Music by Frank Churchill
Additional Lyric by Ann Ronell

Verse

Pre-Chorus

so   he built   his   house   with   twigs.   Heigh   did - dle did - dle,   he
save   the   pig - let   fam - i - ly.   When   they __ knocked __   he

played   on his fid - dle   and   danced   with   la - dy   pigs.   3. Num -   ber
fast   un - locked __   and   said,   "Come in   with   me!"   6. Now   they

three   said,   "Nix   on   tricks.   I   will   build   my   house   with
all   were   safe   in - side,   and   the   build   bricks   hurt   wolf - ie's

bricks."   He   had   no   chance   to   sing   and __ dance   'cause __
pride.   So   he   slid   down   the chim - ney and,   oh,   by __ Jim -'ney, in the

work   and   play   don't   mix!   Ha - ha - ha!   The
fi - re   he   was   fried!   Ha - ha - ha!   The

two   lit - tle,   do   lit - tle   pigs   just   winked   and
three   lit - tle,   free   lit - tle   pigs   re - joiced   and

Chorus

laughed ha - ha!   Who's a - fraid of the big bad wolf,

laughed ha - ha!

big bad wolf,   big bad wolf?   Who's a - fraid of the

big bad wolf?   Tra, la, la, la,   la.

Who's a - fraid of the big bad wolf,   big bad wolf,

big bad wolf?   Who's a - fraid of the big bad wolf?

1.

Tra, la, la, la,   la.   4. Came the

2.

la.

A Whole New World

from ALADDIN
Words by Alan Menken
Lyrics by Tim Rice

with new ho - ri - zons to ____ pur - sue. ____ I'll chase them

an - y - where. There's time to spare. Let me share this

whole new world with you. _____ A whole new

Outro

world, _____ that's where we'll be.

A thrill - ing chase, a won - drous place for you and

me. _____

Zip-A-Dee-Doo-Dah

from SONG OF THE SOUTH
Words by Ray Gilbert
Music by Allie Wrubel